Bedminster's T

A local history project by

Helen Thomas
Rosie Tomlinson
Mavis Zutshi

3rd reprint February 2015

FIDUCIA ✿ PRESS

Thanks to everyone who contributed their memories and experiences to this booklet:

Brenda Aubrey; Patricia Bohin; Mary Bessell; Barbara Giardina; Annie Guest; Beryl Hassell; Jean Hawkins; Dian Keepin; Kaye Lowe; Sher Morgan; Beverly Parry; Pat Pearce; Annette Pearce; Christine Pratley; Jackie Williams; Eileen Willis.

Harold Aubrey; Tony Collingridge; Don Loader; Michael Moore; Lew Pedler; John Powell; Brian Richards.

Illustrations - many of the photographs were provided by the contributors themselves. Especial thanks to Don Loader for sharing his photographs and Dawn Dyer at Bristol Reference Library for all her assistance in locating materials.

The booklet includes images of some but not all of our contributors.

Acknowledgements - Greater Bedminster Community Partnership for £815 funding; the Memories of Bedminster Group for their support and participation; Gemma Geldhart for her encouragement and excellent training; M-Shed for their professional guidance; Robert Wigram, Imperial Tobacco Archivist; Madeleine Hardman, Imperial Tobacco Pensioners Gazette; David Dewhurst of the Tobacco Factory for enthusiastic and generous support for the launch of this booklet.

To Chris Miller and Annie Winner for helpful & perceptive comments on the text and Josie McLellan for her advice and support.

On completion, the materials from the project will be archived with Bristol's M-Shed, creating a permanent record of the lived experience of the women and men we talked with.

Whilst we have focused particularly on women's experiences and contributions in this booklet, we want to thank everyone who so generously shared their memories with us.

Bedminster Tobacco Women Project
For further information please visit our website:-
bedminstertobaccowomen.wordpress.com
If you would like to contribute your own memories please contact us by e-mail:
btwproject@hotmail.com

FIDUCIA PRESS 2014
ISBN 978 0 946217 40 3
Printed in Great Britain by Doveton Press Ltd., Bristol

Setting the scene

The original idea for this project came from Helen Thomas, who had worked during her school summer holidays in the Embassy Voucher Exchange office of the Wills factory in Raleigh Road. Nearly fifty years later, she found herself living in a house whose kitchen window looked onto the now transformed Tobacco Factory Theatre building, and wondering about the experiences of the women who had once worked there.

She realised that many people now living in the area knew nothing of the huge industry that had dominated the skyline of Bedminster for a hundred years or more. Although there are many reminders around the city of the prominence and philanthropy of the Wills family, such as Bristol University's magnificent Wills Memorial building, the City Museum and Art Gallery or the numerous care homes founded by Mary Monica Will's charitable creation, the St. Monica's Trust, there are no similar memorials to the thousands of tobacco workers, the majority of whom were women, whose labour over the decades generated this enormous wealth. Helen and two other local volunteers, Rosie Tomlinson and Mavis Zutshi, decided that one way to create a permanent memorial to these women would be to record, collect and preserve their stories and experiences.

The stripping room

'The Wills Girls', written by Amanda Whittington and performed by Show of Strength Theatre Company in the redesigned Tobacco Factory Theatre in 2002 and 2003, was an enormous popular success. On an academic level, Anna Pollert's book 'Girls, Wives, Factory lives' (1981) highlighted the hard graft and taken-for-granted sexism in the tobacco industry, as well as showing how women developed their own forms of resistance and solidarity. But our main source of inspiration proved to be the sixteen women and seven men whose experiences are recounted here. Those stories reflect the paternalism, the harsh conditions of work and the rigid pecking-orders of class and gender that dominated relationships within the tobacco industry for many years. At the same time, many of them described Wills as a benevolent, progressive employer which took care of its employees and for whom they were proud to work. We have tried to honour the contradictions and complexities of their experiences in this account.

The Wills story originates in the late 18th century when Henry Overton Wills and his then partner Watkins opened their shop selling tobacco imports on Castle Street, Bristol. Forty years later, in 1826, Henry's two sons (H.O. & W.D. Wills) took over what was to become a thriving industry, dominating the tobacco trade & cigarette production in Bristol and subsequently nationally. Ironically, for a family business lauded for its progressive practices and philanthropic activities, its early fortunes were made using tobacco from American slave plantations, until emancipation in 1865 finally ended this trade. For two hundred years, the Wills family ran the tobacco industry in Bristol and its impact on the city and in particular on the suburb of Bedminster was profound.

On the factory floor - 1920's

Bedminster itself is a residential and former industrial suburb located close to the centre of the city. The area developed rapidly from the mid-19th century, first in coal-mining, small manufacturing, leather, glue and paper-making. Later, it supplied workers for the railways and the city's docks and later still, thousands of people, mainly women, were employed in the tobacco industry. The physical reminders of the industry in its hey-day, huge red-brick factory blocks which covered acres of land and dominated the urban landscape from Bedminster Bridge to Ashton Gate, are still here. Today they have been transformed. Number 1 Factory, opened in 1886 in East Street was demolished almost 30 years ago, except for its frontage which now houses the small shops and businesses of Bedminster Parade. Number 2 Factory was demolished and the site transformed by the ASDA supermarket. Number 3 Factory, opened in 1906, is now the well-known Tobacco Factory theatre and cafe/bar on Raleigh Road. Number 4 Factory, further along Raleigh Road, has been replaced by residential accommodation for older people, the land having been donated by the Wills family when the factory closed. Other buildings in Raleigh Road and Upton Road remain but with new uses, while the former Wills Club in Luckwell Road was demolished in 2014.

Bedminster Factories 1 & 2

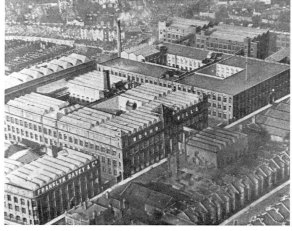

Ashton Factories 3 & 4

Our contributors

Our contributors encompass a fifty-year period. The oldest (Mary Bessell) started work as a 14 year old in 1938 and the youngest (Beverley Parry born in 1961) left the Hartcliffe factory in 1987. It is also a very small group - in total, twenty-three contributors covering a time period in which working life in the industry changed immeasurably. Whilst it's not possible to generalise too widely, their experiences proved to be remarkably similar and their stories create a vivid picture of what it was like to work in this huge organisation.

Most of our contributors, as with the overall workforce, came from the surrounding areas of Bedminster, Ashton and Southville, many of them having lived in these communities all their lives. Their ages ranged from mid-fifties to nearly ninety, with more than half in their eighties. The majority (16) were women but we also talked with seven men, who provided valuable additional insights and alternative perpectives into life in the factories. The majority of the women we talked with had worked on the factory floor for at least part of their time at Wills, most of them starting when they left school (aged 14 or 15 years) in the stripping room. Thereafter, some had worked as cleaners, kitchen staff and cooks. A few had worked only in the offices. Some of the group had come into Wills later, already carrying the dual responsibilities of family and children.

There was a clear distinction between the employment patterns of the women and the men. For example, at least two of the men, Harold Aubrey and John Powell, spent all their working lives in the factory. The latter was given a special certificate acknowledging his 39 years 11 months, since the closure of the factory meant he narrowly missed the coveted 40 years of service. This length of employment was less common among the women with only two of our contributors reaching 25 years or more.

The employer

The Wills empire started its life in 1786 as a small family partnership. It flourished during the 19th century and by 1901, 'it was the biggest and most prosperous manufacturer in the UK' (Birch, 2013). By the 1960s there were 10,000 employees. In 1972 there was a total work-force of 6,000 in Bristol, of whom 4,500 were shop-floor workers, two thirds of them women (Pollert, 1982). When the company transferred its main cigarette production to Hartcliffe in 1974, there were 5,500 employees.

Wills was very much a local company and a 'family business' in both senses of the word, in that it was run by a family and it preferred to employ people from families already working for the firm. It was the major employer in the south of Bristol, with a reputation for being a generous employer and for having a wider philanthropic ethos. Many of our contributors talked to us in their living rooms, often within a stone's throw of the Bedminster factories.

No 1 Factory East St

A family business

'People were so proud to be able to say that they worked for Wills.'
Annette Pearce was talking here about a family tradition - both her grandparents, two great aunts and her parents all having worked for the company. She has in her possession the original document dating from 1914 indenturing her grandmother, then 14 year old Edith Hoskins, to the Imperial Tobacco Company for the next five years to learn the trade of cigar-making.

In 1939, Jean Hawkin's mother decided to get her young daughter into Wills. *'She had never had a child work for Wills and at that time it was quite a prestigious thing to get your son or daughter into Wills, so she worked hard at it'* and after being fattened up sufficiently on war-time rations to pass Wills' stringent health requirements, Jean started there in 1940.

'In those days working in the Tobacco Factory was an accolade. Everybody round here wanted to work there.' Harold Aubrey was referring to 1939 - the

Harold Aubrey

year when he had just left school and war broke out. His mother took him down to apply and put his name on the waiting list.

In 1947, Dian Keepin's auntie, who obviously knew the drill, helped a young Dian to do the piece of sewing that the young women applicants were required to submit, to demonstrate their nimble fingers. It was clearly up to scratch, as Dian was accepted.

Dian Keepin & Jackie Williams

Kay Lowe knew that it always helped if you had a family connection:
'I'd had a couple of aunties that had worked there before... and it goes in your favour if you've got family. When you worked there it's strange how many people there were that were related.'

Even as late as 1970, Sher Morgan told us:
'In the beginning Wills being a family firm, they encouraged relatives, etc to join in, so I had a friend that I went to school with and we all joined Wills at the same time because one of my mother's friends was actually a union rep in Bedminster Wills.'

Sher Morgan

So it wasn't just that there was a 'good family atmosphere' at Wills - it might well have been your family! And parents clearly hoped that their children might follow in their foot-steps. These 'family ties' helped to create a strong sense of loyalty to the company and also meant that the older generation could induct their younger members into proper behaviour at work and then supervise them subsequently - all very helpful for the company and recognised as such.

FIRST TO OFFER CERVICAL TEST

Woman's world

More than 1,100 women at two Wills factories are to be invited to take a test designed to prevent cervical cancer.

A woman doctor and nurse from the Bristol Department of Health and Social Services will visit the medical department at Raleigh Road at the end of next month.

The simple, ten-minute "smear" test will be available free to all women over 25 at the cigar factory, No. 1 factory and the Embassy voucher exchange.

It detects minute changes in the cells of the neck of the womb which might later lead to cancer.

2,500 A YEAR

The sample of cells is taken to Southmead or Bristol General Hospital for microscopic examination and the woman gets the result in about a fortnight.

Cancer of the cervix accounts for about 2,500 deaths in England and Wales each year.

While the highest incidence is in the 35-60 age groups, eleven Bristolians under 35 have died over a five-year spell.

This, coupled with the earlier age of marriage and motherhood, has swayed medical opinion in Bristol towards carrying out the tests on younger women.

Dr. Sarah Walker of the Bristol Health Department told Wills World that it was intended to include No. 1 factory later.

"We hope as many women as possible will take advantage of the test," she said. "It is very simple, painless

Working for Wills

A number of themes which highlighted the complex and contradictory experience of working for an employer like Wills, came through strongly from our conversations.

'It was a lovely firm to work for'

It wasn't just, as Brian Richards explained, that the wages, bonuses and pensions were relatively good (particularly pre - and immediately post-war) until other employers caught up in the 1950's. Nor just that they provided all kinds of additional facilities for their workers ranging from free health care - medical attention, physiotherapy, foot care and dentistry - through to excellent sports and social facilities, subsidised canteens and uniforms. They also supplied a sense of pride - of being proud to be known as 'a Wills girl' - and a comforting sense of being 'looked after'.

Mary Bessell started as an under-nourished 14 year old in 1938:
'When I went in there to work, I was underweight so I had to have cod liver oil everyday and then I went to Keep Fit classes because I was only 6 stone'

And Eileen Willis, who started work there in 1940 put it like this:
'Once you got into Wills, you were looked after. They were very caring, you know, if you had a toothache, you went to the dentist.'

Entrance to the dentist with the toothless lions

This benevolence sometimes extended to family members who weren't employed by the company at the time. Annette Pearce, whose family had the long connection with Wills, told us how her mother got help:

'But before that, before she went to work for them, she approached the personnel lady there, about school uniforms, because they were very expensive comparatively and they actually gave her a grant because my dad had worked for them, they gave her a grant to buy all my school uniform.'

Don Loader

Barbara Giardina, who worked in the canteen, benefited from the support she received to undertake training to improve her qualifications:

'They offered me the chance to go to college because I never ever finished my course so I went to college in Bristol and they sent me on day release. They paid for all my stuff. They paid for all my set of knives and everything.'

Jean Hawkins recalls her husband, who worked in Research & Development for the company, describing the high level of staffing, possibly even over-staffing, in the factory, which was interpreted as an example of 'corporate social responsibility' in action. Or, if not that, certainly of paternal benevolence, common to other national employers with strong local roots.

Jean Hawkins

John Inman entertaining in the canteen

For those subject to the monotony of factory-floor routine like Kay Lowe:
Once a month they used to have, entertainers used to come in and on Friday afternoons there'd be music or somebody telling jokes or singing.'

With the benefit of hindsight, some of the perks were more questionable - everyone received a weekly allowance of forty free cigarettes, which were also offered for overtime, at Christmas, and provided for outings and works socials or for participating in Research & Development trials.

From the perspective of most of our contributors, Wills was experienced as a generous and responsible employer. Harold Aubrey recounted this incident:
'I fell off a wagon and everyday I had treatment from a physiotherapist. The sort of thing that you take for granted when you were working there, but when you look back... Some people's jobs they had nothing at all. But we were extremely well-looked after.'

Life was not all work and the company provided facilities for social and sporting activities.

'We used to have office games, and inter-office matches, and inter-departmental games of cricket, hockey, football... My department, we used to have a Christmas party at the Imperial ground'. Michael Moore.

Perhaps not surprising then, that many of those we interviewed, particularly amongst the older workers, were either indifferent to or struggled to see the relevance of a union during those times.

'It was just taken for granted that you'd go there...'

However the reality was that these benefits did not come without costs. Firstly, there was no choice, especially for working-class 14 year old girls. The same refrain came from nearly all of our women contributors, whatever year they started work:

'I would have liked to have been a hairdresser but things were very poor... And my father was in the war and he was gassed and she had 6 children, so that's where we went, me and my eldest sister.' Mary (started1938)

'And then we came to careers - and I always wanted to do nursing and my father said 'No' and you couldn't do what you liked until you were 21. And the girl in front of me said 'Oh, I'm going to Wills' and I thought 'Oh, I'm going to Wills' and that was that...' Eileen (started 1940)

'There were a hundred and one things I wanted, but not to go into Wills, but anyway, I went...there were quite nice jobs available, which I could have done, had my mother allowed me to, but she didn't.' Jean (started 1941)

'Well, you had to go into Wills where I grew up. They never asked you where you wanted to go. It was just taken for granted that you'd go there.' Brenda (started 1941)

'But I don't think that we were expected to have ambition. I'd always wanted to be a hairdresser, still do. There were lots of things that I wanted to do but I didn't because I always felt held back.' Jackie (started 1959)

'I enjoyed school. I loved it. I wanted to be a nurse. I used to do anatomy and physiology but my step-dad was very strict. I had to start work, I wasn't allowed to stay on at school.' Kay (started 1960)

Nurses in the company library

'*Well, when I left school, I wanted to be a policewoman but my auntie worked there, she said they were taking people on and she got me the application forms and I applied.*' Beverley (started 1978)

'The first day I went home, I cried and cried...'

Despite the benevolence, the day-to-day reality was that working on the factory floor was hard, if not harsh, work.

'*They were very strict. And there were rows of like desks in there and you sat down and you had a tub on one side and your eighty bundles on this side and you had to do eighty-two pounds - and you'd start from the beginning and strip the leaves off the stem and make sure there was not a bit of tobacco left on the stem and if there was, you did it all again.*' Mary (1938)

'*Your first introduction to Wills was the hand-stripping room, so I went into the hand-stripping room and the smells of tobacco and lots of people, quite overwhelming really, when you're fourteen, so I was very, very nervous! I wasn't happy.*' Jean (1939)

'*Anyway, it was bitter January. And my dad used to leave home at 6.30 am and you'd just come out of school, you know. Anyway you went in the factory and it was stripping leaves. And, oh your fingers, they did bleed. You had to strip all the leaves off because that was the value of it. Anyway, I used to come home crying. I didn't like it.*' Brenda (1941)

'I remember the girls, you know, rows and rows of girls, with canvas bags, and they were stripping away, they had to do x number of pounds or bags a day, and it was very labour-intensive in those days, and all the machinery was done by belt drives, so it was very different.' John (1945)

'In those days the tobacco came in hogs heads, they were about 4 foot round and that high... they were made of wood... the tobacco leaves were like cabbage leaves, they were like that, massive, but by the time they finished [production at Raleigh Road, in 1984] it was like privet leaves, because it was all stripped abroad and just came in cardboard boxes, ready for use. Yes it changed over the years.' John (1945)

'It was very very hard to the point where my sister said to my mum, 'You can't let her go in there. It'll kill her!' I was like really puny - a tiny little thing.' Jackie (1959)

It was all done on bonuses, you had to have everything weighed, so the longer time you took to drink your tea, the less time you had to strip the leaves and get them in the basket to get them weighed and you'd lose out on your bonuses.' Kay (1960)

Annie Guest worked in Wills on the factory floor 'under cover' for a year in 1979. She was then a social scientist from Bristol Polytechnic (now UWE), exploring the viability of setting up a degree in management relations. She observed the work at close hand and was struck by how demanding it was:

'It was a very skilful job that those girls did. It wasn't anything automatic that you could just shove a machine into the string and cut it... because the leaves were all different shapes and sizes and sometimes the vein instead of being straight was skewed, but you still had to cut it to get the vein out and not spoil a whole leaf.' Annie

Annie Guest

From the stripping room, you might move on to the 'beating-up' room where the dry tobacco leaves were threshed and prepared for feeding into machines to make hand rolling tobacco or the 'washing-down' room - all hard, unpleasant manual labour.

'Do you remember the washing-down room? My sister worked there. She had a Sou'wester like the fishermen and a great big raincoat. She was only fourteen, mind. They had to wash the tobacco down and when that pusher used to come in, that stuff was all caked up. And the smell never goes - it goes into your skin.' Dian (1947)

'We used to have the brig where the tobacco come in, we had to split they open with a crowbar. It was hard work mind. They was like squashed together and we had to put them through this brig and at the other end they'd come out all steamed... Sweat was running off you.' Pat (1968)

Cigar making

Waitresses in the staff canteen

Those who worked in the kitchens, like Barbara Giardina also described a tough regime:

'It was damned hard work the kitchens, the catering was hard. I don't think the factory people worked so hard. They always seemed to be having tea-breaks. But we did obviously because we were catering for so many people.'

Kay Lowe who inherited her cleaning job from her mother, recalled one particular charge hand:

'...who was so strict on her cleaning. Everything had to be done precisely and exactly. You couldn't cut any corners and... you're given specific jobs to do, like cleaning all the skirtings or polishing all the wood doors, and after you did it, the charge hand would make sure you'd done it right.'

As mechanisation was introduced and the tobacco arrived already stripped, the degree of repetitive or sheer physical labour required on the factory floor decreased but it was still hard and monotonous work for many.

There was tremendous loyalty to the firm which management recognised:

'Both women and men, would do the same job for 30 or 40 years with no apparent resentment. Many of these people would be the kind of people who got up at 4 in the morning if snow had been forecast to see whether there was going to be a problem, and if there was they set out walking. And there were people there who hadn't been late for 40 years and were very proud of that. Quite rightly so.' (Tony)

Getting on at Wills

There seemed to be few routes up the promotional ladder for the women we talked with and it was difficult to get a sense of how women who wanted to could have progressed from the factory floor or cleaning, to other kinds of work within the company.

Jackie Williams would have liked to have become a Wills Guide like her friend, showing visitors around the factory:
'It didn't happen every day, but it'd be a couple of times a week or it'd be your turn. You'd train up and you'd get extra money.'

One route was by getting qualifications as with Barbara Giardina who was able to move up the kitchen ranks to become a pastry chef.
'Anyway I passed my catering thing. It was really good. I had credits... I had really high. So they gave me a chance to go on the pastry, which is what I like, so from then on I stayed in the management dining room.'

But as a woman, you might also have to put up with the every-day sexism that went along with putting yourself forward. One of our contributors was sent on a course to learn how to be a supervisor and found herself the only woman there. She had to do a verbal presentation to demonstrate her ability to speak in front of a group:
'I said, "Oh God, what am I going to talk about?" And he said, "Don't worry. Just wear a tight jumper. Stand up there and make it prominent and we'll all be looking at it".'

Factory guides

Although most of our male contributors had been promoted during their working life, essentially this meant waiting your turn - Brian Richards who was active in the union aptly called it 'dead men's shoes, for a brown coat'. The other way to advance yourself, he said:
'...was to be in The Wills Club. Lots of them used to go up there on the basis,"We'll get on in Wills if we belong to the Club." ' The Club refers to the firm's social club that male employees could join.

Brian Richards

For management, however, to start with there was a clear route to promotion, but sometimes career decisions were simply a matter of chance, as Tony Collingridge remembered:
'I worked up through the ranks of production manager in various factories, then a departmental manager, then an assistant factory manager, and then, rather unusually for a 'cigarette man', all of a sudden I was sent for and informed I was going to be the factory manager of the cigar factory in Raleigh Road. There was no formal succession planning either. It was just "Oh, we need a new factory manager, who's around?" '

Gender and class hierarchies in the factory

'We were looked down on then, the women, the factory women, but as the years went by, you were nearly all equal.'

For all its benevolence and paternalism, the Wills company was run along strictly hierarchical lines. Pat Bohin's comment above nicely sums up how the pecking order worked - and how this changed over time. But long after many other companies had modernised their staff/management relations, Wills maintained its traditions of deference and hierarchy, by a number of means.

Dian Keepin remembered her father's tales of working life below stairs in the days before the Second World War:
'My dad was a hall porter there. He used to clean the managers' shoes under the stairs. and it was all "Sir" this and "Sir" that.'

Don Loader, the Wills photographer for many years, still has photographs of the impressive tobacco factory buildings with their carefully graded and separate entrances, staircases, washrooms and eating facilities.

Pat Bohin

He described the army of women cleaners, whose daily tasks included polishing the floors of the famous 'rubber corridor' where the portraits of the management hung, cleaning out their coal fireplaces and burnishing the silver and gold cigarette boxes on the desks till they gleamed.

Eileen Willis reflected on how, as an office worker, she was expected to behave with the other ranks:
'But I was told that I only had my job because 'they' were working, so they said "Don't get big-headed. They're only like you. You wouldn't be here, if they weren't". Which is true... but from telling you that we relied on them, they did keep you separate. And you weren't expected to marry anyone from the factory, the boys weren't expected to get interested in the girls. It was a real class divide.'

John Powell described the contradictions he observed:
'They looked after everybody and yet everybody was segregated. Because the cloakrooms were all segregated, as well - factory men, factory women, supervisors in another entrance, junior management in another, senior management was another...'

John Powell

The senior management had their own dining room, complete with a kind of ante-room where gin and tonic was served every day before lunch. Kay Lowe remembered doing a casual shift in the bosses' dining room:

'Everything was upmarket, it was grand, the meals were absolutely amazing. Everything was first class, top class, the best of everything, the special chef that used to cook all these specials. It was a different world but it was lovely.'

As Barbara Giardina explained:

'When you were cooking for management you could have what you liked. You could say to Tony "Could you get some venison, could you get this or that?" and we would have it. It wasn't like that in the main dining-room. You had to work to the penny.'

'Canteen was for the factory, restaurant was for the staff and the management canteen had a management staircase and they lived entirely differently. We didn't use the one with carpet on. Carpet was for management!' Eileen

'Because the cloakrooms were segregated as well, factory men, factory women, supervisers in another entrance, junior management in another, senior management was another, so it was all sort of in little compartments.' John

The staff canteen was amalgamated, but the factory, yes, you had all men and all women, and the only time they went together was at Christmas time, when they had a Christmas sing-song or carols, probably they had the school round doing carols, that sort of thing.' John

Directors' dining room

As an up-and-coming manager, Tony Collingridge didn't always respect these separations of rank:

'Ah, the management staircase! I actually started using it before I was entitled to. But the head porter had evidently decided I was going places and not just upstairs so he didn't rebuke me for it. I didn't know!'

But he also enjoyed the privileges:

'And when you got promoted to whatever level it was to join the directors in their dining room, you got a silver napkin ring with your initials engraved on it, as well as the label on your door, and all that.'

Even when the whole operation moved to the new modern factory in the 1970s, the separation continued:

'At Hartcliffe they still had a separate dining room for management, because their dining room was separate in the management offices'. Beryl

The net result of these distinctions was to create separate worlds whose boundaries were not to be crossed.

'You didn't wander far from your own department' was how Eileen, then working in the offices, put it:

'and when you did go into the factory through a narrow passageway, you always had this feeling that you were crossing over'.

Management entrance

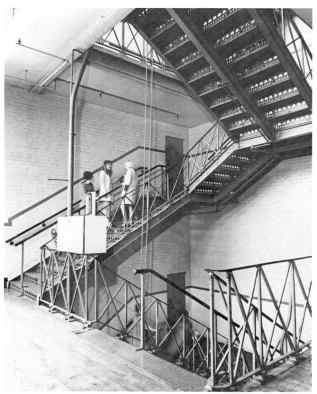

Factory stairs

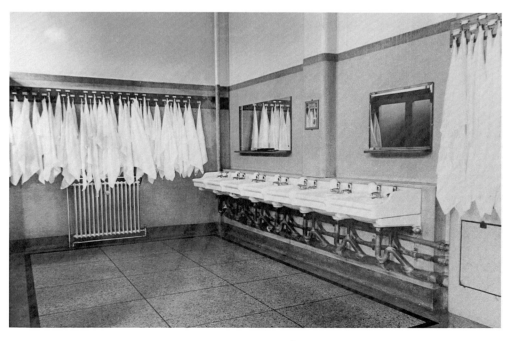

Management washroom

It worked the other way too. Kay Lowe remembered the feeling of inferiority it created in her:

'When you're younger and you see all these big bosses going around with all their suits, all smart, you think "My goodness, I can't speak to them" because you're lower than them.'

Sher Morgan expressed similar feelings:

'It was more reverential years ago. If a manager would walk round, very rarely would they speak to you. They were nothing to do with you. They were above your station. They weren't really hands-on. You just knew they're somebody important.'

But the young Eileen Willis was unimpressed with the hierarchical structures:

'The boss stopped his car as I was coming through Queens Square and asked me if I'd like a lift to work. So I got in and he was chatting away. And when I got to work, they said "You came in Mr So and So's car!" I was supposed to be very honoured but to me it was just a lift to work. I suppose I was a bit Bolshie really, I hated all this hierarchy!'

Maintaining discipline

There was a well-developed system of regulation within the factory, which was kept in place by supervision and control, from clocking-in procedures and sanctions for lateness, through to having to raise your hand and ask permission to go to the toilet, from not being allowed to go to other parts of the factory to wearing different coloured overalls for different grades of staff, from reviews for inappropriate behaviour through to regular searches of employees for stolen goods, especially cigarettes.

'You didn't get anything for nothing. It was well paid, they did look after you, but it was very strict. You couldn't get away with anything, really.' Jackie

'Everybody used to have to clock-in and you only had to have a couple of lates and you were up on the carpet. It was quite an accepted strict discipline.' Brian

'When you went out of the factory, and they could pick anyone out to be searched, a full, like, body search, not take your clothes off, but they just used to body search like that to make sure you didn't take anything out you shouldn't have done.' Kay

'And then another thing they'd do on an evening on your way out, you'd have to go downstairs and the supervisors were there by the door to check you to see if you were pinching anything and, of course, they'd pick on some of us all the time. We'd get pulled in every night of the week for five nights.' Barbara

There were particularly strict rules about bringing cigarettes from outside into the factory.

'You were allowed so many cigarettes. I'd been on holiday for a fortnight and I had two left in a packet that I'd bought, and I used to smoke one before I'd start work. I don't know why I didn't smoke the other and I went through a barrier and the thing went off. And they called me in. Now I'm in a grey coat and I was searched and it terrified me. "Why did I have that cigarette on me? Where did I get it?" Beryl

A few of our contributors mentioned the fact that the punishment for stealing cigarettes was instant dismissal, including the loss of the invaluable pension, no matter how long you had worked for the firm.

Factory canteen

Working women

Working women in war time

Some of the women we talked with had experienced working at Wills during the Second World War or had seen the aftermath of the war when men returned and reclaimed their previous roles.

'I can remember having to go into the cooling room in the war. There was somebody up on the half-deck pushing down the tobacco and us filling up the trolleys'. Mary

'When I went into the cigarette-making there were women still manning the machines, because they did the men's jobs during the war and you also had the feeling that you

were intruding a bit. They'd been there a long time, old staid women. And there was a lot of spinsters there, because of that reason I think they felt it was their domain a bit - they had a bit of power.' Jackie

'And there was a lot of spinster girls there as well, among the older women, but they were the fall-out from the First World War, when there were not so many men for girls to marry, and Wills employed a lot of older single women. And gave them a lot of consideration and support.' Michael

'All the married women, when the war ended, married women had to leave, because the men were coming back and wanted their jobs back.' Eileen

'Men's jobs were done by women during the war, they did sort of double-up, you know what I mean, if there was one man, there was two women. A lot of the women done the men's jobs, and as they came back from the forces they just went back to women's work.' John

Marriage and motherhood

As with many other employers, including the civil service and local government, women were expected to resign from their jobs at Wills when they got married. This continued until the late sixties, although some of our contributors found ways of staying on until they were expecting their first child. Subsequently they had to give up their jobs on having the baby. Wills' benevolent approach to employment practices did not extend to maternity leave provision. Whilst the men might expect to have a job for life, most of the women we talked with left Wills on their marriage or at the birth of their children.

'I left when I was pregnant with my son in 1956.' Dian

'You left when you got pregnant. They didn't keep your job open, not like now. You had to get your pension out.' Jackie

'Well, they wouldn't take people back... I don't know, they had this unwritten law that you couldn't go back if you were married.' Eileen

'My mother worked there when she was single, but of course, once you got married, you had to stop.' John

So the women's employment patterns tended to be less continuous, often with shorter periods of employment in different parts of the factory. Whilst the catch-phrase of 'a job for life, a good wage and a cigarette allowance' was theoretically true, it didn't actually apply if you happened to be the one having babies. However, later on the company modernised its approach and it became possible for women to come back or join Wills, once their children were older.

They still faced the familiar problem of combining the demands of work and child care. Barbara Giardina's description of managing the combined roles is a familiar one:

'How I managed life around it I don't know, because I had two small children growing up. Luckily my husband was on shift work and I had a sister-in-law living in the street, so between them... I think my daughter was probably about 5 or 6 when I started in there and she was a very very sensible girl, she'd go to school and I could give her the key.'

Barbara Giardina

Later still the company introduced more flexible shift patterns:
'They had shift working, they had part-time working, and they also had school-hours working. Yes, girls could go to work at 10 o'clock and leave at 3. They took the children to school and collected them afterwards.' Michael

And managers could sometimes be sympathetic to the difficulties faced by women workers dealing with pregnancy. Tony Collingridge recalled:
There was an older woman, late 30s perhaps, who got pregnant, and there was a great deal of trouble taken to keep that a secret because of the stigma still associated with getting pregnant as a single woman'.

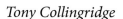

Tony Collingridge

Supervisors and managers

Although women outnumbered men in many sections of the shop floor workforce at Wills, all the women we talked with occupied subordinate positions. We heard from some of our contributors about the female charge hands and supervisors, but only one woman manager (in Human Resources) was mentioned. Lew Pedler who joined the company in 1968 could recollect one female Management Trainee who happened to be a woman, and ten years later, another who became an Assistant Departmental Manager. And, as with any group of workers who find themselves at the bottom of the heap, they were sometimes scathing of the men who worked alongside them, supervised or managed them.

'What did your husband do in there then?' Beryl
'Like all the men in there, nothing! What I would say though, that of the men in there he

was one of the better ones. It was the women what done the work. The men were there just to maintain the machines and, you know, parade about.' Beverley

Annie Guest was shocked at the lack of relevant experience of many of the university-educated managers:
'I said to him "What did you do at Oxford or Cambridge?" He said "Classics". I said "But what good is that to you when you're on the shop floor and looking after workers?" And he said "Well I know how to be with people". And I said "But you don't know how to deal with any of the problems that arise on the shop floor, do you?" '

'My mechanic was never there. He'd start the machines up at twenty to eight, at Hartcliffe not down here, and then he'd go for a tea-break for half an hour, come back for twenty minutes and then off again.' Beverley

There were some tales of male bullying and harassment:
'We had a nasty supervisor. Oh, he was a pig. I was doing my training when I was at college, he decided he'd help train me as well! He came in the kitchen and said "Right, I want you to do these onions and I want you to chop it like this, all in little pieces, you know small, not just rough chopped". So he brought two sacks in and I had to chop all these onions. I was crying. It was awful. I think it just went to his head that he had the supervisors job and he came back after and I said "I've finished now", and he said "They're not good enough" and he dropped them all in the stock pot and he said "Now do another lot." Barbara

Top packing room

Even those destined for senior management had to learn the ropes on the factory floor. Tony Collingridge joined the Wills management training scheme in 1957 after doing national service in the navy. He recalled:

'Part of the training, for example, was after we had been taught how to do it, we were put in charge of the production output from one cigarette-making maching, and we spent six weeks doing that and leaning quite a lot in the process'.

Young managers with the wrong attitude could find it difficult to get on with the factory workers:

'If you were at all posh, know-it-all, you had a hard time, and some of them did. One of our trainees, who was an aide-de-camp to some high-ranking general during his service time, he got tipped into this thing when he reached down to get an armful of tobacco. I didn't see it happen, but I know it happened. He was too la-di-da, and he had a completely contrasting view of how you enjoyed your time in the making-room'. Tony

How women perceived the union

Several unions operated in the tobacco industry at different times, including the Transport and General Workers Union (TGWU) and the Tobacco Workers Union (TWU) and the Tobacco Mechanics Association (TM). Production workers could belong to either of these unions. However, as Lew Pedler explained, there were significant differences within the production process that affected how unionisation operated:

'The primary area, preparation and blending the tobacco, was the dirty end of production. It was wet and dusty. The secondary area where final packing happened was much cleaner. The primary area was lower status, lower paid and lower skilled. The secondary area was more organised and powerful and where unionisation was strongest.'

However, despite the fact that women in manual occupations were increasingly joining unions in the late 1960's and early 1970's, amidst a national climate of heightened industrial action, Wills had enjoyed relatively strife-free relations in the early to mid-70's. It was in the late 70's and early 80's that the primary area of production became more militant and organised. Although there were female shop stewards in the union at Wills during this time, most of the women we talked with had had little active involvement, in what was widely seen as the province of the men. Union membership itself was historically encouraged by the company, as was frequently the

Beverley Parry

case in large and paternalistic organisations.

Dian Keepins' anecdote is a telling one in this context:

'We used to have a party down Wills Recreation and that year we went on strike, old Bennett he got up on the stage and told us "You're very lucky to have a party this year because you went on strike".

The simple question 'Did you belong to a union?' revealed another division in the workforce. Eileen Willis talking of her experience of working in the company offices in the 1950's, told us:

'The staff were not in a union. No, definitely there was a "them and us" '.

But for Beverley Parry working on the shop floor in the 1970's, it was clear cut:

'Yes, you had to be, didn't you?'

Other women, who had experience of the Hartcliffe factory, were supportive of the union:

'Yes, they were always pretty busy with working conditions and health and safety, it was good to have that kind of thing. And when a lot of things were being automated, the unions would step in and say "Well, you know you're doing away with somebody's job". In those days, with unions, you'd need to have the union behind you. Although sometimes it got too militant and they were too big for their own good. In the end, the theory of having a union representative, you never know when you'll need that.' Sher

'So anyhow they got the union leader and she said "We've had enough of this. Come on. We're going up to the office". And they changed it. And there was uproar really, at first from changing it and I wasn't liked for it, but they did change it.' Pat

But Jackie Williams saw it as representing narrow and sectional interests:

'It was alright at the beginning. There were the big unions, but by the '80s it did change. They did want more, not so much for us but the electricians, they got greedy.'

Beryl Hassell was reluctant to get involved:

'When we went up to Hartcliffe, the two union women were packing it in and the foreman, he called me in and asked me how did I feel about taking over the union. And I said "No". I told me dad and he said "Leave that alone, my girl. Don't go fighting other people's battles".

Although there had been a one day national stoppage

Beryl Hassell

of Imperial Tobacco in the 1970's, those who could recollect it were hazy about the reasons for the strike:

'I suppose it would have been for more money I don't know, or cut backs. Isn't it funny, you see, I can't remember, I don't know if anyone else could tell you. We never felt... I mean we used to get production money. We used to get that, as well, if the factory done well, we had that on to our wages as well. I can't remember what it was about. The whole factory went out but it didn't last very long. It must have been about wages.' Barbara

She described how divisive it had been:
'I can remember when the factory went on strike, we in the kitchen decided we weren't going to strike with them so we all went in and this particular morning they were all waiting there and they threw eggs and flour and all sorts at us – the factory staff. They called us all traitors.'

Although some of the women recognised that the union was necessary, particularly in latter years, their sense of identity and solidarity seemed to stem far more from their informal networks and the different ways they found to support one another.

Fun, camaraderie and solidarity

One of the strongest themes that came through our conversations was how, despite the monotony and boredom of tiring and repetitive factory work, despite the strict and sometimes petty disciplines imposed by a hierarchical system of charge-hands, supervisors and managers, people managed to have fun at work. The close physical conditions of working life, the set-up of small teams of women working as cleaners or in the kitchens, or grouped around their machines, created positive collective experiences, and forged friendships and bonds of solidarity that were described with great affection. Many of our contributors had found both their partners and life-long friendships through working at Wills. A group of Wills women who meet regularly at

the local Hen and Chicken pub, still sit with the same women with whom they sat in the canteen forty years ago.

'It was wonderful. It really was as I said. Like I said it was blooming hard work but I can't ever remember waking up and thinking oh I've got to go in that place again except when that supervisor started.' Barbara

'There were rows and rows of seats in the canteen, and everybody, the camaraderie was amazing. And the friendship that you developed well, I just can't explain it. The youngsters of today, it's so sad that they don't know that. They've got no idea that they can make friends.' Kay

'But Bedminster was lovely to be. Everybody, almost anybody that you could have found would say the atmosphere of Bedminster was lovely.' Pat

'So I ended up working in the wages office over in Bedminster. I went from Ashton over there and I loved it. I thought I could never do it but I made lovely friends there. I've got lovely photos of when we were all together.' Mary

'I did move on from that job. I worked in reception and I've had a few different jobs but unless I could've been a hairdresser I wouldn't have changed it, because of the generosity of the people that worked there and later on the more human attitude of the management, even.' Jackie

'A lot of the women seemed older. They were like mothering you, sort of helpful and in some ways they became your friends and you'd all go out in a big gang and have a laugh and then it didn't matter about ages eventually.' Sher

'But that was the thing about whether you could always have a good laugh out of anything serious. That was what it was like in factories, wasn't it?' Beryl

There was certainly plenty of messing about:

'It was always a bit of fun. Always. The young ones we used to cover for them

31

and they'd be off with their girlfriends when they'd finished the work upstairs in the empty rooms up there with their girlfriends and things like that. We'd have to sneak up and tell them to quick get back because the supervisor's looking for them. It was real good fun.' Barbara

'Oh, I mean health and safety would have a field day now, but in those days you could get away with things especially when someone was getting married or there was a maternity and they do funny little things for them. And sometimes the great big bins of tobacco waste when they were empty, someone would push you in and you couldn't get out because you couldn't lever yourself out. You'd be stuck in there and they'd hear a little voice saying 'Help! I can't get out.' Sher

'We had the song in the kitchens [sings] "We are the Will's girls". Have you heard it? I don't know if it was just for the kitchen but we had our own words anyway, because we said "We know our manners, we pay our rent, we are respected, wherever we did go... When we're walking down Raleigh Road, doors and windows open wide, then you hear old Phyllis shout, get the bloody dinners out!" You know, she was a great big fat woman our supervisor then and that was our own song. I didn't realise they had it in the workshops as well. They must have put their own words to it and that was always sung at all the parties.' Barbara

And it went beyond just fun to stories of generosity, mutual support and finding ways to resist the management:

'But again talking about peoples' generosity, to get the annual bonus, you'd have to be there at the start, like March to March, so say like me, I started in August you didn't get any, then they'd have a whip round for you. Sometimes you'd get about £6 or £7 - and they might only have £20!' Jackie

'If the men had, if their wives had babies, they used to string up a thing and put papers

on to look like nappies. And they used to bang, all the sections in our general office, they had six sections, and they was, it was all metal sides, and they used to bang the doors, it

did make a racket. But they used to give them presents, for babies. That was it, they had a baby, and that was it, it was acknowledged.' Eileen

'So the girls would be frantically stripping. I wasn't very good at it, in fact I was a terrible book-worm at the time, and always, always reading, so the girls used to say "Tell us about it", so that was the start, and every day, that was me, sitting there, stripping tobacco, telling them about my book that I read, so you can imagine, they were all stripping away and I was telling my story and going slower and slower [laughs] so every day I didn't do my weight of tobacco, so the girls used to help me, they used to give me a little, so I would never get a bonus, but I always had my weight.' Jean

'I couldn't work the treadle and put the leaf in at the same time, I cut the vein, I just couldn't do it. They said to me "Oh, the foreman's coming and we'll get into trouble". And they didn't know who I was, I was just another worker as far as they were concerned, and they thought they were helping me by showing me how to do it properly, which I wasn't doing properly.' Annie

Things that kept everybody laughing and joking were important but so were the acts of solidarity, resistance and subversion, that allowed the women to feel that they were still individuals with their own views and identities, not simply compliant factory workers:

'There was one manager that they didn't like, so they made, they bought a present for him, and I was horrified when they showed me what it was, it was a rubber penis. They wrapped it all up very carefully with a big bow and all the rest of it, and they didn't say anything to him, they just said "It's a present there for you, sir". Annie

'How about a Friday, then? You'd put your hand up to go to the toilet. Brenda would be in there and she'd do your face for you.' Dian

'But yes, on their days off they used to go up to the Cabot Tower, well one or two of them who had their day off would go up to the top of the Cabot Tower with a white flag, and they'd have a pre-arranged time with the women workers in Wills, and they would keep saying,"Can we go to the toilet?" and they'd disappear up to the roof, and they'd come back down and somebody else would go. They signalled to one another from the top and they thought this was hilarious.' Annie

'This particular night Julie came in and she was expecting and we could see that she is not very well, so all the rest of us covered for her because they used to walk round, the supervisors, checking that you were doing things and someone would give you the eye when the supervisor was coming.' Pat

Wills leaving Bedminster

Tobacco was arguably the main industry in South Bristol for much of the 20th century, employing upwards of 10,000 people at its heyday in the 1960s. But as time went on, increasingly fierce competition between the major tobacco companies and changing technology led to significant changes. Tony Collingridge recalled:
'Part of it, the Players companies decided to get rid of the old factories and build a huge

Hartcliffe factory under construction

Moving out

new one. That outflanked Wills, and Wills didn't like it. And there was an easy solution to that: build one yourself. And we did. I don't think it was economically justified. But it was partly justified. The sheer speed at which you could make cigarettes went from, including filters which was a brand new concept then, it went from 600 a minute to 10,000 a minute.'

Tony recognised, however, that Wills had been slow to deal with the opportunities offered by greater mechanisation even in the old factories, although the unions had been unwilling to accept change:

'We didn't tackle... on our cigarette machines, we had one operator and one catcher-girl, absolutely unnecessary to have them both. Players had two of the same machines to the operator, and we had one. And try as we would, we couldn't get the union to agree to it'.

So in the late '60s Wills began to plan for a modern factory to replace the out-dated facilities at Bedminster and Ashton. The company hoped to move a new site at Ashton Vale, but when the city planners blocked this, they began to develop a huge new complex at Hartcliffe. Everybody was affected: travel-to-work patterns, the machinery, working routines and staffing levels all changed.

Not surprising then, that in the memory of our contributors, the relocation of the tobacco industry from Bedminster to the Hartcliffe site in the mid 1970's had a devastating impact on the local community:

'When we moved to Hartcliffe, they say East Street, I'm talking about the '70s, lost a good £100,000 a week in trading. Because the girls all used to go out to shop in the lunch hour.' Michael

'And when it went to Hartcliffe, they had nothing. I mean they had a little Post office, a little shop, but that was nothing like going out into East Street. All you could do up in Hartcliffe was walk round the grounds. Bedminster had everything. It killed Bedminster when Wills went. You can't imagine it was Wills now, if you go down there. I don't think of that when I walk through the arcade now. It's so grubby and everything.' Beverley

It was clear that a 'golden age' of cigarette consumption was finished by the end of the 1970's, with increasing public awareness of the health risks and increases in tax. The Hartcliffe factory, which was billed as Europe's largest cigarette manufacturing plant, only remained in operation for a further sixteen years and the whole site was sold off by 1990.

Then and now

The Ashton tobacco factory still dominates North Street. What used to be the historical centre of the neighbourhood, which provided employment for generations of families and linked it so closely with the local community, has since been transformed into a lively artistic, cultural and social centre. It also generates employment and income, although on a much more modest scale and brings people from all over Bristol to the south of the river.

In Bedminster, the massive ASDA supermarket has replaced the Number 2 Factory. While the imposing facade of the original Number 1 factory and the company offices still dominate East Street, the imposing corridors and vast factory spaces which used to lie behind the red-brick frontage have gone, and been replaced by bland new buildings which house small shops and anonymous businesses.

The history of the tobacco industry is full of contradictions. As we know now, without any doubt, it is responsible for producing one of the most individually and socially damaging products that exists. Paradoxically, it was also one of the most publicly charitable industries in the history of the city, making handsome bequests to Bristol University, funding the building of churches, hospitals and other public facilities and providing employment to thousands of people from Bedminster and across the city.

For many of our contributors, working at Wills was seen one of the best times of their lives and they regarded themselves as fortunate to be 'Wills Girls'. At the same time, the work on the factory floor at the primary end of production was often hard and dirty, and these women were at the bottom of a rigidly segregated organisation. Despite their role in creating the wealth of Bristol's tobacco industry, their contribution remains almost completely unacknowledged. As with many other industries dominated by women workers, their experience is invisible - 'hidden from history' in Sheila Rowbotham's classic phrase. They deserve much better than this.

References

Simon Birch - The archaeology of the cigarette industry in Bristol. The Elephant in the Room. MA Dissertation, University of Bristol, 2013.

Anna Pollert - Girls, Wives, Factory Lives. Macmillan Press, 1981

Sheila Rowbotham - Hidden from History. Pluto Press, 1973

Picture credits
Don Loader - pages 3, 7, 10, 11, 13, 14, 16, 20, 21, 22, 24, 27, 35, 39
Bristol Record Office - pages 4 & 5
Wills World Magazine - pages 8, 9, 12, 15, 17, 19, 30, 31, 32, 34

Websites
www.bbc.co.uk>Bristol>History
www.bristolpast.co.uk Tobacco - The Changing Face of Bristol
www.imperial-tobacco.com Imperial Tobacco Group
www.mshed.org - Transforming Places of Work
Davenapier.pwp.blueyonder.co.uk - WD & HO Wills Tobacco Manufacturer - History & Timeline
itv.com Tobacco Industry Downfall - ITV news Tues 6 March 2012

Fiducia Press is a non-profit making community publisher specialising in local and social history, transport and poetry. For a full book list contact the address below.

fiducia@blueyonder.co.uk

Bedminster Tobacco Women Project
For further information please visit our website:
bedminstertobaccowomen.wordpress.com
If you would like to contribute your own memories please contact us by e-mail:
btwproject@hotmail.com